SPORTS' WILDEST UPSETS

OLYMPIC GAMES UPSETS

HEATHER RULE

Lerner Publications ◆ Minneapolis

Lerner Publications Company
An imprint of Lerner Publishing Group, Inc.
241 First Avenue North
Minneapolis, MN 55401 USA

For reading levels and more information, look up this title at www.lernerbooks.com.

Main body text set in Aptifer Sans LT Pro.
Typeface provided by Linotype AG.

Library of Congress Cataloging-in-Publication Data
ISBN 978-1-5415-7712-1 (lib. bdg.)
ISBN 978-1-5415-8964-3 (pbk.)
ISBN 978-1-5415-8366-5 (eb pdf)

Manufactured in the United States of America
1 – CG – 12/31/19

CONTENTS

Every Olympic athlete dreams of standing on the podium with a medal.

OPENING CEREMONY

ATHLETES WORK HARD TO GET TO THE OLYMPICS. They practice for hours on end for their chance to win an Olympic medal. That opportunity only comes every four years. Some athletes only make it to the Games once. Others might be past their prime competition years by the time they return. They want to make their Olympic moment count.

But one of the most exciting things about Olympic sports is that they're unpredictable. Superstars can make unexpected mistakes, and low-ranking athletes can have the best performance of their lives. These upsets make the Olympics that much more exciting.

Sometimes, the upset will end the winning streak of a champion on a softball field or beach volleyball court. Other times, victory will take a little bit of luck on a sheet of ice in speed skating or a hockey game.

FACTS AT A GLANCE

- The US men's hockey team was young and inexperienced at the 1980 Winter Olympics. Their opponents were the Soviet Union, who had won the previous four gold medals. Team USA beat the Soviet Union in a historic 4–3 win.

- Australian Steven Bradbury used a strategy to beat the odds and win gold in **short track** speed skating in 2002. Skating in the far back, Bradbury pulled ahead when all of his opponents fell in a chain reaction. Bradbury's unexpected victory shocked many.

- Czech skier Ester Ledecká became the first woman to win gold in two different sports when she did so at the 2018 Winter Olympics. She upset defending champion Anna Veith from Austria in the super-G alpine skiing event and also won a gold medal in snowboarding.

LONE OLYMPIC LOSS

AMERICAN KERRI WALSH JENNINGS EXTENDED HER OLYMPIC BEACH VOLLEYBALL RECORD TO 26-0 DURING THE 2016 OLYMPICS. She and her previous partner, Misty May-Treanor, had won 21 Olympic matches, only losing one Olympic set during their 11 years together. Now competing with partner April Ross, Walsh Jennings was two wins away from a fourth gold medal.

Agatha Bednarczuk (*left*) blocked a shot from Kerri Walsh Jennings at the 2016 Olympics.

Barbara Seixas became a hero after she and Bednarczuk brought home a historic win for Brazil.

Many expected Walsh Jennings and Ross to beat their Brazilian opponents in the 2016 semifinal in Rio de Janeiro, Brazil. Instead, the women found themselves in an unfamiliar position. They had lost the first set 22–20. Now they were facing **match point**.

Opponent Agatha Bednarczuk finished with a **kill** that bounced off Ross and out of bounds. Brazil won 21–18. Bednarczuk and teammate Barbara Seixas jumped up and down. On the other side of the net, Walsh Jennings put her arm around Ross.

It was the first time Walsh Jennings lost a beach volleyball match at the Olympics. She and Ross won the bronze medal that year instead of gold.

FINAL MATCH SCORE

BRAZIL | USA

2 | **1**

Before meeting Rulon Gardner (*right*) at the 2000 Olympics, Aleksandr Karelin had not lost a match since 1987.

KARELIN DETHRONED

AT THE 2000 OLYMPICS IN SYDNEY, AUSTRALIA, EVERYONE EXPECTED ALEKSANDR KARELIN FROM RUSSIA TO WIN IN GRECO-ROMAN WRESTLING. Karelin was a 286-pound (130-kg) heavyweight champion with an 887–1 record. He was looking to win his fourth gold medal in a row.

Karelin was up against American Rulon Gardner. Karelin tried everything he could to score a point. He tried to lift Gardner off the mat, but Gardner kept his hands and feet touching the ground.

At one point Karelin's hands came apart from their grasp. Gardner was awarded a point. Karelin tried for another **reverse lift**. But Gardner held his ground. Every time Karelin tried to score a point, Gardner wouldn't let him succeed.

In the final seconds, Karelin put his arms down in defeat. Gardner raised both arms and did a somersault on the mat to celebrate his unlikely gold medal.

Gardner had never placed higher than fifth place in world competitions before defeating Karelin.

DOWN ON THE FARM

Gardner didn't get his strength from spending hours in the gym. He built his muscles working on his family's 160-acre (65-hectare) dairy farm in Wyoming, baling hay, hauling rocks, and carrying pails of milk.

MIRACLE ON ICE

THE 1980 OLYMPIC WINTER GAMES TOOK PLACE IN LAKE PLACID, NEW YORK. The US men's hockey team was playing against the Soviet Union, a nation that included Russia and existed from 1922 to 1991. The United States and the Soviet Union were a mismatch in hockey. The Soviets had won the past four Olympic gold hockey medals. The United States had the youngest group of players at the Olympics.

The United States lost to the Soviet Union two weeks before the Olympics. Many thought they would lose again in Lake Placid.

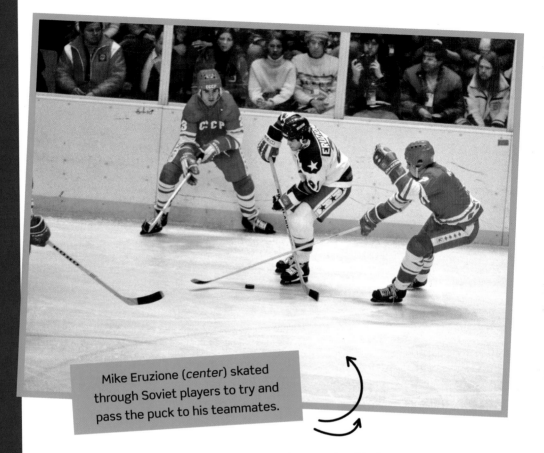

Mike Eruzione (*center*) skated through Soviet players to try and pass the puck to his teammates.

The Soviets had the best players in the Soviet Union— maybe even the world. Few thought the United States had a chance to win.

Behind 2–1 in the final seconds of the first period, American Dave Christian shot the puck 100 feet (30 m) toward the goal. The puck found its way to teammate Mark Johnson, who scored one second before the period ended. Then the Soviets took the lead again in the second period.

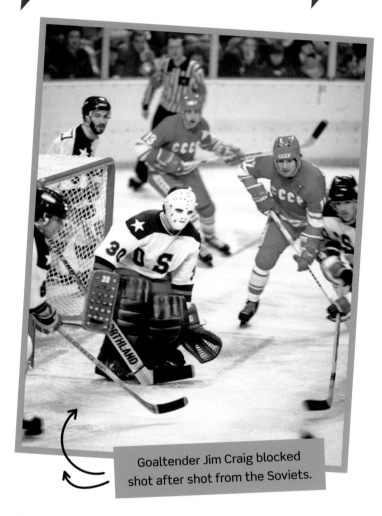

Goaltender Jim Craig blocked
shot after shot from the Soviets.

The United States tied the game for a third time with a goal
in the third period. With 10 minutes left in the game, Team
USA captain Mike Eruzione gathered a loose puck and fired
a low shot past the Soviets' goaltender for a 4–3 lead. It was
the only lead the United States had all game.

The Soviets pressured hard to tie the game. But Team USA goalie Jim Craig stopped every shot. The fans in the arena counted down the last seconds of the game. ABC TV broadcaster Al Michaels couldn't contain his excitement either. His call as time expired—"Do you believe in miracles? Yes!"—is one of the most famous in televised sports.

The crowd roared. The US players rushed onto the ice to celebrate. Team USA clinched the gold medal two days later with a win over Finland. But the victory against the Soviet Union was the true miracle on ice.

Team USA players embraced each other on the ice after their incredible win against the Soviet Union.

FINAL SCORE

USA | SOVIET UNION
4 | 3

Sarah Hughes began skating when she was three years old.

A HUGHES UPSET

SARAH HUGHES WAS NOT EXPECTED TO WIN A FIGURE SKATING GOLD MEDAL AT THE 2002 OLYMPICS. She was only 16 years old. Many thought her US teammate Michelle Kwan would win. Hughes was in fourth place after the first part of the skating competition. Kwan was in the lead.

Hughes was first up in the **free skate**. She started her routine with four triple jumps. She landed every single jump almost perfectly, spinning quickly in the air and then touching her skates gently back on the ice.

The young skater finished with a fast spin in the middle of the ice, her arms above her head. She ended the spin and stuck her right skate behind her. She smiled and waved to the crowd.

Then Hughes waited for the results. She jumped from fourth to first in the standings. When everyone was finished skating, she was still in first. Hughes had won the gold medal! She and her coach screamed with joy when they heard the incredible news.

Hughes celebrated her incredible upset with her coach Robin Wagner (*left*).

"LOOK AT MILLS!"

AMERICAN RUNNER BILLY MILLS WASN'T EVEN CLOSE TO THE RUNNERS AT THE FRONT OF THE PACK. He was so far behind that people watching the race on television couldn't see him toward the end of the men's 10,000-meter race at the 1964 Olympics.

Mohammed Gammoudi (*center*) tried to edge in front of Billy Mills (*722*) during the 10,000-meter race.

Mills set an Olympic record in 1964. He completed the 10,000-meter race in 28 minutes and 24.4 seconds.

On the final lap, Mohammed Gammoudi from Tunisia was in the lead. Then Australia's Ron Clarke, who was expected to win, closed the gap on Gammoudi.

Suddenly, Mills sprinted past Clarke and Gammoudi in the final 30 meters (98 ft.). A broadcaster for NBC TV started screaming, "Look at Mills! Look at Mills!"

Mills raised both arms when he ran past the finish line. He gave a big smile and waved to the roaring stadium of fans. Mills became the first American to win an Olympic gold medal in the 10,000-meter event.

ANOTHER OBSTACLE FOR MILLS

Mills was diagnosed with hypoglycemia. He had low blood sugar. He didn't know if he'd be able to finish the race. His historic victory and his life inspired the movie *Running Brave*. It was released in 1983.

The US softball team competed against Japan for the gold medal in Beijing, China.

JAPAN ENDS USA'S SOFTBALL RUN

THE US SOFTBALL TEAM CAME INTO THE 2008 OLYMPIC GAMES WITH THREE STRAIGHT GOLD MEDALS. It wanted a fourth. The team's chance came against Japan on August 21, 2008.

The game was tight. Japan's Eri Yamada smashed a home run in the fourth inning. That gave Japan a 2–0 lead. The United States kept things close. American Crystl Bustos hit a home run to make it a 2–1 game. But Japan scored again in the seventh.

Japan's Yukiko Ueno went back to the pitcher's mound in the last inning. The first out came when a Team USA player popped a ball foul, which was caught. Then Ueno got the next batter to **line out** to third base. Caitlin Lowe was the last hope for Team USA. She connected and hit the ball. But third baseman Megu Hirose made the throw to first to end the inning and win the gold.

SOFTBALL: YOU'RE OUT!

Softball was first added to the Olympics in 1996. In July 2005, the International Olympic Committee (IOC) decided to remove it from the Olympics after 2008. Then in 2016 the IOC voted to add softball back in starting in 2020.

FINAL SCORE

JAPAN | USA
3 | **1**

ALL-AROUND CHAMPION

AMERICAN GYMNAST CARLY PATTERSON WAS IN EIGHTH PLACE AFTER THE VAULT DURING THE WOMEN'S ALL-AROUND COMPETITION AT THE 2004 OLYMPICS. She moved into fourth place after the uneven bars. Patterson needed near-perfect routines on the balance beam and floor exercise if she wanted a shot at a gold medal. Also standing between her and the gold was superstar Svetlana Khorkina. The 25-year-old Russian already had two Olympic gold medals.

Carly Patterson was the top gymnast for the United States in 2004.

Patterson nailed her somersaults on the beam. She took a deep breath before her dismount. She landed firmly on her feet.

She did so well on the balance beam that she moved from fourth place overall into first. But she still needed to have the floor routine of her life in order to get a gold medal. She jumped high in the air and landed perfectly on her tumbling passes.

Patterson clinched gold, becoming the first American woman to win the gymnastics all-around gold medal since 1984.

Patterson was only the second American woman to win the all-around competition at the Olympics.

Steven Bradbury's (*300*) chances of winning the 1,000-meter short track final looked more and more unlikely after each lap.

LAST MAN STANDING

AUSTRALIAN SPEED SKATER STEVEN BRADBURY KNEW HE COULDN'T KEEP UP WITH THE OTHER FOUR SKATERS IN THE MEN'S 1,000-METER SHORT TRACK FINAL. The 2002 Olympics were Bradbury's third, but this was the first time he had made it past the quarterfinals of this event. In the final, Bradbury and his coach decided to let the others skate ahead of him. This would let Bradbury take advantage if other skaters in front of him fell to the ice.

That's exactly what happened. China's Li Jiajun tried to pass American Apolo Anton Ohno on the outside with two laps to go. He didn't make the pass. Jiajun created a chain-reaction crash. The four lead skaters tumbled to the ice toward the outside barriers.

Bradbury was the last man standing. He crossed the line first before anyone else could get back on their feet. Coming into the race, Bradbury was the underdog. Then he won Australia's first gold medal at an Olympic Winter Games.

Bradbury became known as "the accidental hero" after his win.

DREAM TEAM DEFEATED

THE US MEN'S BASKETBALL TEAM HAD BEEN KNOWN AS THE DREAM TEAM SINCE THE 1992 OLYMPICS. It had the best players in the world. Going into the 2004 Olympics, the United States had won all five previous games against Puerto Rico. Few thought that would be different when they met again in Athens, Greece.

The 2004 US men's basketball team included top National Basketball Association (NBA) player Dwyane Wade (*left*).

But Puerto Rico gave the Americans a challenge. They played solid defense. Puerto Rico led 49–27 at halftime. Carlos Arroyo was the star for Puerto Rico and continued to score.

The United States tried hard to come back in the fourth quarter. But Arroyo wouldn't let them. He sank a running layup with less than five minutes left in the game. As the clock continued to count down, the Puerto Rico players knew they had the win. Arroyo finished the game with a team high of 24 points.

Puerto Rico won 92–73. It was only the third loss in 112 Olympic games for the US men's basketball team.

Carlos Arroyo led Puerto Rico to the upset.

FINAL SCORE

PUERTO RICO	USA
92	**73**

MIRACLE ON SNOW

ESTER LEDECKÁ STARTED 26TH IN THE SUPER-G ALPINE SKIING EVENT IN THE 2018 OLYMPICS. The top medal contenders had already finished. The Czech skier bolted from the starting gate at the top of the mountain. She hit each gate and gained speed as she got closer to the bottom. She was flying on her final jump toward the finish line.

Her final time was .01 seconds ahead of defending champion Anna Veith from Austria. Ledecká stood with her mouth open in shock at her gold-medal finish. A camera operator told her she won. Ledecká shook her head and said, "How did that happen?"

The super-G gold medal was Ledecká's first podium finish at an international skiing event. Her real talent was in snowboarding. She also won her snowboarding event, the parallel giant slalom, that year. She became the first woman to win gold medals in two different winter sports at the same Olympics.

Ledecká kissed her gold medal after she won the super-G skiing event.

CLOSING CEREMONY

WHETHER IT'S A GAME, ROUTINE, OR RACE, THERE IS ALWAYS POTENTIAL TO WATCH A STUNNING UPSET UNFOLD AT THE OLYMPIC GAMES. The athletes that compete at the Olympics are the best of the best. They had to work hard and focus to make it to the world stage.

Emotions run high when an Olympic gold medal is on the line.

A loss can be devastating to an Olympic athlete, especially when it is unexpected.

But sometimes these Olympic athletes need more than experience to get to the top of the podium. Sometimes, they need a little bit of luck. There's no doubt that there will continue to be Olympic upsets in the future. Stay tuned to the Olympics to see which athletes might see their dreams come true.

SOURCE NOTES

13 *USA Today*, "Remember When? Team USA Defeats the Soviet Union for the 'Miracle on Ice,'" 7 May 2019, https://www.usatoday.com/story/sports/olympics/2018/02/08/remember-when-team-usa-defeats-soviet-union-miracle-ice/1052092001.

17 *The Washington Post*, "After 50 Years, Billy Mills's Olympic Gold-Medal Moment Still Being Felt," 8 May 2019, https://www.washingtonpost.com/sports/othersports/after-50-years-billy-millss-olympic-gold-medal-moment-still-being-felt/2014/10/26/2525f1da-5be3-11e4-8264-deed989ae9a2_story.html.

27 *MPR News*, "'This Must Be Some Mistake,' Says Snowboarder After Winning Olympic Gold in Skiing," 8 May 2019, https://www.mprnews.org/story/2018/02/17/this-must-be-some-mistake-says-snowboarder-after-winning-olympic-gold-in-skiing.

GLOSSARY

all-around competition: the Olympic event in which gymnasts compete in every gymnastic event and then add up their scores

free skate: the second of two parts in a figure skating competition, in which skaters have more time to perform their routine

Greco-Roman wrestling: a type of wrestling in which wrestlers may not use their legs for attack or defense

kill: in volleyball, a hit that directly results in a point

line out: a play in baseball in which a player catches a ball that is hit powerfully and parallel to the ground

match point: a point that could result in one player or team winning the match

reverse lift: a move in wrestling in which one athlete is on his hands and knees and the opponent grabs him under the stomach, flipping him up and over to the opposite side

short track: a speed event skating that takes place on a smaller track and involves multiple skaters competing

FURTHER INFORMATION

Doeden, Matt. *Coming Up Clutch: The Greatest Upsets, Comebacks, and Finishes in Sports History*. Minneapolis: Millbrook Press, 2019.

Herman, Gail. *What Are the Summer Olympics?* New York: Grosset & Dunlap, 2016.

Ignotofsky, Rachel. *Women in Sports: 50 Fearless Athletes Who Played to Win*. New York: Ten Speed Press, 2017.

Olympic Games
https://www.olympic.org/olympic-games

Rulon Gardner Moves into Coaching Wrestling
https://olympics.nbcsports.com/2018/05/14/rulon-gardner-wrestling-coach-high-school

US Hockey Hall of Fame
https://www.ushockeyhalloffame.com/page/show/831562-the-1980-u-s-olympic-team

INDEX

PHOTO ACKNOWLEDGMENTS

The images in this book are used with the permission of: © CP DC Press/ Shutterstock.com, p. 4; © Jamie Squire/Getty Images Sport/Getty Images, pp. 6, 7, 14, 25; © Neal Simpson - EMPICS/PA Images/Getty Images, p. 8; © Billy Stickland/ Allsport/Inpho Photography/Getty Images Sport/Getty Images, p. 9; © Focus On Sport/Getty Images Sport/Getty Images, pp. 10, 11, 13; © John Kelly/Getty Images Sport/Getty Images, p. 12; © John MacDougall/AFP/Getty Images, p. 15; © AP Images, p. 16; © Bettmann/Getty Images, p. 17; © Jonathan Ferrey/Getty Images Sport/Getty Images, pp. 18, 19; © Clive Brunskill/Getty Images Sport/Getty Images, p. 20; © Corey Sipkin/New York Daily News Archive/New York Daily News/ Getty Images, p. 21; © Timothy A. Clary/AFP/Getty Images, p. 22; © Gary M. Prior/ Getty Images Sport/Getty Images, p. 23; © Andy Lyons/Getty Images Sport/Getty Images, p. 24; © Alexis Boichard/Agence Zoom/Getty Images Sport/Getty Images, p. 26; © Javier Soriano/AFP/Getty Images, p. 27; © Phil Noble/PA Images/Getty Images, p. 28; © Al Bello/Getty Images Sport/Getty Images, p. 29

Front Cover: © Doug Pensinger/Getty Images Sport/Getty Images, top left; © Jonathan Ferrey/Getty Images Sport/Getty Images, top right; © Alexander Hassenstein/Getty Images Sport/Getty Images, bottom.